Cracking Open

*a creative journal
for self-transformation*

Molly Carroll

MA, LPC

Illustrations: Molly Carroll
Cover Art: Mary Jo Hoffman Designer: Paige Barnes
Author Photo: Natalie Plus

Table of Contents

"Your problem is how you are going to spend this one and precious life you have been issued. Whether you're going to spend it trying to look good and creating the illusion that you have power over circumstances, or whether you are going to taste it, enjoy it and find out the truth about who you are."
~Anne Lamott

To Begin...

I was 28-years-old, living in San Francisco, teaching third grade, and the world as I knew it was falling apart. Unbeknownst to my family and friends, I was getting ready to elope to Las Vegas with my Italian boyfriend so that he could get a working visa. Then, suddenly, one day I woke up and realized I could not marry this man. We could not be together. I knew deep down that I was not in love with this man and could not make this massive mistake that would affect the rest of my life. This would be challenging for anyone, but I feel like it was extra hard for me because I had convinced myself that this gangly girl with freckles and pale white skin from Omaha, Nebraska had hit the jackpot with this gorgeous Italian architect from Milan. But I knew I had to do the thing I most wanted not to do: end the relationship.

I was devastated, crushed, and massively heartbroken when I did so. I remember sitting in my therapist's office sobbing when she looked at me and said, "In this moment you feel like your white picket fence is crumbling." She hit the nail on the head. Indeed, the life I thought I was going to live, being married, having children, living in two different countries, was crashing around me and I was fully cracking open. I was forced to wake up to the reality that life wasn't always going to go as planned and that I had to face my pains and heartaches head on. With the help of my therapist, I saw this crisis as an opportunity to learn and grow. Yes, a door was closing, but something was opening too, cracking open, and I had to be fully present to the possibilities before me, that I could, would, love again; that all my personal and professional goals were still possible; that I could even still live in Italy if I wanted!

Part of the reason I became a therapist was to help other people who find themselves at a similar crossroads in life, where they feel stuck, overwhelmed, and/or surprised at the hand life has dealt them. I knew at a young age that I was a searcher, drawn to people's stories of triumphs and tragedies, always magnetically pulled to helping others in their pain, becoming an educator and therapist is in my DNA. I have spent over 20 years schooling myself in the educational and psychological fields. I have started two after-school programs for children to help them with self-esteem, confidence, body image, and social skills. And currently I have a private practice where I guide families and children to discover what helps them grow, transform, and make positive change in their lives. I share my experience and credentials with you because I want you to trust me to guide you on this journey of cracking open. What I believe makes me most successful in helping others is that I recognize I need help as well.

As a searcher and a quest seeker, I have gone to all the darkest corners of myself, and to the many corners of the world to find growth and healing. I have done everything from years of personal therapy to traveling to India to have a personal audience with His Holiness the Dalai Lama. I have spent hours in a Catholic confessional and spent weekends with shamans and healers, all to find the answers to my purpose and a connection to the self. The result of this extensive journey has been profound lessons in life, love, and spiritual growth, which I want to share with you.

Perhaps you aren't able to devote your life to seeking and understanding these questions as I have, but that's okay, because I've done a lot of the work and research for you and in this book I offer answers, guidelines, and tools to help you not feel so alone, to find your purpose and to heal the negative behaviors and thoughts that inhibit you from having a deeper connection to others and stand in the way of your happiness.

So why this book? Why now?

Why would you want to leave your world of comfort, "rock your emotional boat," and enter into a world of mystery? I believe something drew you to this book and it means your heart is ready to crack open and you are ready to find the inspiration you need to change your life. You are ready to **BE** something more and by entering these **BE** chapters you will.

Perhaps, you've been told to push through the tough times, to keep a stiff upper lip, told not to let others see your weaknesses, to not dwell, etc. If all of this advice is supposed to make life easier, why doesn't it? Because it's what others want from you, it's not what's best for you. What's best is to walk through your life being vulnerable and honest about who you are and how you are feeling. To reach out to professionals, friends, and loved ones when you are feeling lost and alone, to not be afraid of needing a hand to hold. What's essential is to allow yourself to be open to change and transformation, and ultimately not to follow anyone else's rules in life, but to learn to listen and trust your own inner wisdom. What do you get from living this way? Simply put, a happier and more fulfilling life!

This book's purpose is to help you get comfortable with the uncomfortable. Because let's face it, life isn't comfortable or easy most of the time. My Dad used to say, "life is full of challenges and how happy you are depends on how you deal with each one." My goal is to take all of my beautiful and awful experiences, as well as my years in therapy and years as a therapist, mother, and friend and give you the tools you need to wake up and live the life you should be living. You might say it's twelve days, weeks, or years of therapy in twelve chapters.

How will that happen?

Cracking Open is about grabbing your pen, pencil, crayon, or marker and reading each of the chapters with an open heart and mind, then taking the time to creatively ponder and answer the questions I have provided for you. Through my guidance and your introspection you will discover your deepest truths. By reflecting on the thought-provoking questions in these pages, you can learn how to go deeper into your own experiences, knowing that this is where true inspiration lies. This book will be an arena for you to be honest, to be completely transparent, maybe for the first time in your life. I've also included valuable tools I've used as a therapist for you to integrate into your daily life to create more happiness. By answering the questions with courage and using the strategies I have provided I wish for you to become fearless and relish in new discoveries and wisdom.

While reading and engaging with this book, you will also develop and enhance your creative spirit. This journal is meant to be written in and painted on, so dog-ear the pages, spill your food and drink onto them. It is a book to be lived in; it is an experience to be had. By doodling, sketching, and coloring you will learn to let go of your long laundry list of chores in order to play and find your child-like spirit leading you to greater happiness.

Not that this process will *always* be fun or easy. Reflecting upon your life can sometimes be messy, ugly, and painful, but it can also be meaningful, enlightening, and rewarding. It is only by taking a full measure of who you are, where you've been and what you want to do, that change is possible. Transformation is a journey. There is no starting point and no final outcome, just lessons to be learned and re-learned, applied and re-applied. Sure, sometimes you'll get frustrated. In those moments, you will learn when to keep pushing and when to throw your hands in the air and say, *I can try again tomorrow*. The one rule is don't hold back or censor yourself. Rather, immerse yourself in this piece of art with complete openness and honesty, make these pages yours, have fun, play, share your heart and soul and walk away a clearer, happier, and more compassionate human being.

So grab this book and take the time to sit down with your favorite beverage (tea, café, wine, kombucha) in a cozy chair with a warm blanket, day or night, and indulge in your own life, crack open your own world.

As William Shakespeare wrote for Antony and Cleopatra, "The breaking of so great a thing should make a greater crack."

It's time to begin... Let's get cracking.

Draw, paint, or write here what needs to "Crack Open" in your life.

Be Awake

Shortly after the Buddha left his temple he was wandering down a path when a man came up to him and said, "You look like some handsome prince," which he was. "Are you some kind of God?"

"No," said the Buddha.

"Are you some kind of wizard or magician?"

"No," again replied the Buddha.

"Are you a human?" the man asked.

"No."

Then the man asked, "What are you?"

The Buddha smiled and said, "I am awake."

I heard this story told by Jack Kornfield, renowned Buddhist teacher and author, and in this one profound statement — "I am awake"— the Buddha teaches us so much about how we can live. *Awake.* Living in a place of awareness of all that is around us each and everyday. Awake to our fears, foibles, confusions, and sadness. Awake to our gifts, graces, and gratitudes. Awake to what is authentic in our hearts. Awake to embrace what your body and soul was put on this planet to do.

To be awake often means we need to step out of our world of routine and amenities and step into a world of uncertainty. It means that you cannot always play it safe and that you have to push your boundaries of comfort to really feel alive. To be awake means to really live in the here and now.

I believe something drew you to this book and it means your heart is ready to wake up and you are ready to find the inspiration you need to change your life. By going on this journey I am asking you to trust what I am saying, and more importantly, trust yourself in hopes of change. When you delve into your internal world of emotions it is inevitable you will gain consciousness.

There are three practices you can implement into your life to become more fully awake. **They are living with intention, not numbing your feel-**

ings, and facing your fears. These three practices will help you participate in the world awake versus asleep.

Awake.

I was 38 years old when I received a phone call from my sister that awoke me to my core. She said, "Molly, Dad just had a massive heart attack." This heart attack began a two-year battle that included several infections, two strokes, and eventually took his life. But it was this phone call that woke me up. I instantly hopped on a plane to travel to my childhood home in Nebraska to be with my family. While on the plane I had this overwhelming feeling that life is really precious and it can change in an instant. I was faced with the truth that we have no control over life and that we must be awake to fully live. It is disheartening that it takes illness and loss to wake up, but it is with these challenging moments that we are face to face with the depth of our emotions, forcing the body, mind, and spirit to stop and only focus on the present moment. With the illness and loss of my father, I woke up and could think of nothing else but my father. I made a promise to myself to try to live every day with intention.

Living with intention looks like mindfully making choices about who you spend your time with, what you put into your body, and how you spend your hours and days. Living with intention is about consciously making choices out of wants and needs versus shoulds and coulds. It is about watching what thoughts fill your mind, because how you think directly affects your every emotion. Living with intention is about choosing a life that you love and respect in order to create happiness and contentment.

The one exercise I want to share with you is something you can do everyday. It takes very little time, so you can do it while taking a shower or working in your office, while driving your car or washing your dishes. It is about asking yourself a question that involves seven words, "How can I live with intention today?" After asking yourself this simple question listen intently to the answer you may hear. Do you hear "Live with more patience or joy, with more rest or play?" Or you may hear "You need to speak up more or begin to listen to others." When you ask yourself this question you become more conscious about daily choices verses going through life on autopilot.

Once you start living with intention you will have more access to your emotions and recognize when you chose to feel an emotion or when you chose to numb an emotion. Have you ever felt emotionally numb? As if all your feelings have disappeared? You are not alone, we have all felt this way, and the beautiful thing about being awake is becoming aware about how you numb your uncomfortable emotions in order to not feel. Numbing emotions can look like everything from over-eating to taking drugs and drinking to excess. It can involve compulsive shopping or an overdose of TV or video games. It is about doing anything to get away from being in your body.

Brene Brown, American scholar and author shares, "There is a full spectrum of human emotions and when we numb the dark, we numb the light." Beautifully said, when you numb the emotions around jealousy, anger or rage you numb the emotions around joy, happiness, and love. Start looking at how you use numbing agents to not feel, and remember that isn't the whole point in life to feel?

Ask yourself, why do I numb my feelings? Why am I so afraid to feel? What will happen if I truly feel my dark emotions?

Begin today to notice how you numb your emotions in order to not have to face the dark and uncomfortable feelings around your trauma, sorrow, and grief, and stop today.

Lastly, to be awake you must start to face your fears. One of the scariest moments in my life was getting on a plane to travel over 6,000 miles to Dharmasala, India, to volunteer with Tibetan refugees and attend the teachings of the Dalai Lama. I was leaving my husband, 7-year-old son, and 5-year-old daughter to adhere to a calling. My fears revolved around leaving the comforts of my home and country to travel alone in a foreign land for three weeks. Yet somewhere deep down inside I knew in order for me to fully awaken and not be limited by my fears, I had to travel to India and start living more in my heart and not in my fears.

Generally, facing our fears comes down to looking at death. Why we keep ourselves imprisoned is because we are afraid to die. We are scared that if we do something that really scares us we may not live through the experience. But this is the key: when we face death, we truly awake to living.

We face our fears so that we can awaken our heart, to stay alive and vital to whatever comes our way. Each time you face one of your fears you awaken to your strength and build your foundation of resiliency. You start to discover that you are stronger than you imagined and can handle more challenging situations than you ever thought was possible. This belief system of facing your fears will awaken you to a more vibrant life.

You deserve a dynamic life; it is your birthright. In order for this to happen it is imperative that you take time to look at your unhealthy behaviors and habits that don't serve you anymore. The Dalai Lama speaks of this journey of self-awakening, "Where does a happy world start? From government? No. From United Nations? No. From individual." My father taught me that a happy world starts when you start to wake up to what your life is all about: living with intention, not numbing your feelings, and facing your fears. Not that it will always be easy, but it is essential to be happy.

It's tempting to stay safe in your nest of protection around your comforts and routines. But I would rather follow the advice of Tibetan Buddhist nun and author Pema Chodron, "To be fully alive, fully human, and completely awake is to be continually thrown out of the nest." So jump out of your nest and allow yourself to not be afraid to wake up to the life you were meant to live. This catapulting experience will teach you to trust the answer when others ask you, "Who are you?" You can answer as the Buddha did, **"I am awake."**

Awake

AWARENESS: Let today be the day that you finally become aware of how your fears stop you from living.

Write three things, in different colors, that you are afraid of and how you can start to overcome these fears.

A**W**AKE

WONDER: Wake up to the wonders of the world. Be in a space of curiosity, about who you are, and where you want to go.

Make a wall of wonder with pictures that spark your curiosity and inspire your soul. Don't be stuck in your adult box, bring out your childlike spirit.

AW**A**KE

APPRECIATION: On the days that you are feeling down, think of all the people, and gifts life has given you.

Appreciation lifts you out of your slumber, and wakes you up to the gifts in your life. Write down three things or people you appreciate in your life and why.

AWAKE

KEEN: Have the ability to think clearly about your life.

What numbing agents do you put in your body, or surround yourself with, in order to not face your choices and decisions? Where in your life do you need to wake up?

AWAK**E**

ENERGETIC: By staying active and exercising you will have an awakened spirit. You will approach each day with intention, a more positive outlook, and clearer mind.

Today move your body by going on a walk, doing some yoga poses, or running after your kids. Notice how different your body, mind, and spirit feel when positive energy pulses through your body. Write on this page how you feel after exercising.

Come with me on this journey...

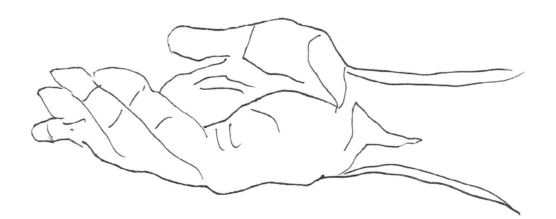

All you ever
owe anyone
is the truth

Be Lost

"Be patient toward all that is unsolved in your heart and try to love the questions them-selves like locked rooms and like books that are written in a very foreign tongue. Do not now seek the answers, which cannot be given you because you would not be able to live them. And the point is, to live everything. Live the questions now. Perhaps you will find them gradually, without noticing it, and live along some distant day into the answer."
~Rainer Maria Rilke, Letters to a Young Poet

I remember the moment my father died as if it were yesterday. I watched as his frail body stopped breathing and the machines stopped beeping, leaving a deafening silence in the room only broken by the sobbing of my siblings and mother. I was in my childhood home, with all my loved ones and surrounded by all that was familiar. Yet, all I remember is the acute sensation of being lost, of feeling like I was floating in the world without a touchstone or anchor. For months I was lost in the grief, and sadness, with the knowledge that my life would never be the same.

When you think of "being lost" what comes to your mind? Maybe your memory traveled to a time as a child when you lost your mom at a department store, unable to see her through all the racks of clothes or when you wandered around looking for a destination that you just couldn't find. Or, perhaps, you thought about it in a more metaphorical context. When you graduated from high school or college and felt unsure about the direction of your life or career. Maybe, right now, you are lost in negative patterns that are not serv-ing you, eating, drinking, or shopping, indulging too much—God knows we all love to indulge too much at times. Or you feel lost in your career or life, dreadfully bored in your routine of waking up, making lunches, getting your kids to school, going to work, coming home, doing laundry. The relentless schedule and cycle of errands may cause you to wonder:

"Why am I really here? What is my purpose in life?"

Like wandering a dark road with no GPS, being lost can feel terrify-ing and you want to rush to find the nearest exit. But cracking open is about actually allowing yourself to be fully lost and immersing yourself in the dark spaces of the unresolved questions in your heart because when you are able to surrender to the bewilderment of your life, you begin to discover who you are. You may be asking yourself, "Why would anyone want to stay in a state of feeling lost which causes pain?" Because the only way to find your light is to experience what Swiss psychiatrist and psychotherapist Carl Gustav Jung, calls "the dark night of the soul."

"The dark night of the soul" is a term to describe a time in your life when you are surrounded by darkness — divorce, death, disease - where everything is lost and it appears as if you cannot go any deeper into your pain. It is a time when nothing makes sense and your life feels meaningless and as if it is collapsing. The dark night of the soul is a death of sorts, but what is dying is your concept of what you thought your life would be. And with each death comes a rebirth. A beautiful part of "the dark night of the soul" is that with patience and time comes light. Jung states, "There are as many nights as days, and the one is just as long as the other in the year's course. Even a happy life cannot be without a measure of darkness, and the word 'happy' would lose its meaning if it were not balanced by sadness." It is about allowing yourself time to hear the dark cries of the soul and when you listen you will begin to find your light. I am not saying this is a "walk in the park" it is hard as hell, but by being lost and diving deep into these emotions and giving yourself time and space to hear the answers to fundamental questions you may have been asking for years, you will find a deeper meaning of your life.

Let's look at it another way. Each day is met with the rising sun and morning light and each evening is met with the dark sky and the wise moon. The human experience is also the same. We cannot have light in our life without the dark. Yet despite knowing this is a natural occurrence, we fight the dark. We do this because it isn't fun to be perplexed or disoriented in our lives, it feels scary and confusing. But once you understand that it's necessary and inevitable, and even beneficial, you can stop fighting and trust that this dark place of confusion will soon lead you to discovery. Thoreau said it best, **"Not until we are lost do we begin to understand ourselves."**

Why is being lost so challenging? Being lost is really about change. When you feel lost in your life you are being forced to change something you are comfortable with and we as humans do not like to be uncomfortable. When we are children our brains are still developing and so we are more comfortable with adapting to change, and as we age we encounter more difficulties processing change because our brains become less plastic and our patterns are more ingrained.

So my first piece of advice for when you feel lost is to take residence there for awhile, live in the unknown and learn to use your body as a compass to direct you home. Practically speaking this means stopping for five seconds just to breathe, writing in your journal about your feelings, taking a walk and allowing your tears of confusion to flow freely, or attending a meditation retreat for several days. Whatever the method, be patient and take the time to become aware of how you react when you're in this space. It is during this time of reflection you can ask yourself these questions.

What behaviors do you exhibit when you are vulnerable and not in control? How uncomfortable are you in not knowing your next steps? What words come out of you when you feel fear creep into your life? Do you become manic? Go into denial? Numb out?

It is this investigation that leads you to know and understand yourself that much more deeply.

As a therapist, one of my best tools is to encourage clients to ponder their purpose and investigate their hopes and fears, as I am helping you do in this book. But often they say, "Just tell me what to do. How can I fix this?" And I respond, "I would a pretty ineffective therapist if I just told you what to do." My job is to help quiet the negative voices while guiding you through your darkness, so you can find your own solutions.

Recently, I had a client who had been lost and frustrated with her job for months. During our sessions we spent a lot of time delving into the reasons why she was unhappy; her boss was micromanaging her, she felt as if she was just pushing paper, and she wanted more time for herself. One day I asked her if she could just be lost in all of her frustrations for just a few minutes and sit quietly, meditatively, yet awake and ask herself, "What should I do now? Why am I unhappy in my career?" As she took time to close her eyes and sit peacefully she began to share that she was feeling a stirring in her belly and a pull in her heart that was saying, "You are unhappy because you are unfulfilled. It's time to move on." When she was able to sit peacefully with her thoughts, she was able to hear her inner voice, which crystallized her predicament and then allowed her to take next steps accordingly. It was, for her, an important turning point. Ram Dass, author and spiritual teacher shares, **"The more you become quiet the more you hear."**

This may sound simple, to sit and listen to what your inner voice, your gut, needs to tell you, but it is actually incredibly challenging in our fast-paced, 24-hour media-driven lifestyle. It is not only technology that makes this difficult, it is life. I am a working mom with two children, a sister to four siblings, a friend, oh, and a wife. Life is busy; it just is. That's why it is imperative to carve out the time to do so, by turning off the TV, the phone, the computer and turning inward. It is no small task to take the time to listen to your inner guide, and have faith that the answers you hear to these soulful questions are your deepest truths, but it's vital.

My second piece of advice is to trust that you will not feel lost forever. Think back: have you ever been stuck in an emotion forever? No. They shift and change all the time. I have the most beautiful view out my office window. I can see the flowing Deschutes River, the magnificent Cascade mountain range, and have the gift of an eagle and osprey nest in arms reach. I spend a lot time everyday witnessing the changes of the natural world, from the snowy cold winters to the blazing summer heat; the hard untilled soil blooming into a colorful spectrum of flowers. Watching these seasonal changes assures me that the natural world does not stay the same, and nor will we. As author Albert Camus said, **"In the depth of winter, I finally learned that within me there lay an invincible summer."** As the seasons change I am also reminded to change as well.

This is the lesson for all of us, that being in the dark spaces of bewilderment is a natural state and if we can just breathe and rest assured that it will change, we will be okay. I know you want to run away and distract yourself so that you feel anything other than the sticky black tar emotions you're experiencing, but in these moments say one of my favorite biblical mantras from Corinthians, "This too shall pass. This too shall pass." Then soon, like the first buds of spring, you will start to feel a shift of lightness and warmth. I have a client whose boyfriend had ended their relationship and she was absolutely heartbroken. She wanted to fill the dark spaces of pain with anything, a new job, a blind date, shopping, or food. And she asked me, "What can I do with all this pain?" I suggested that this is the time to give the pain some space, and in doing this it will lead you to healing. If you just replace the pain with distractions it will reside in the body and resurface at another time. Trust that these emotions that are so painful will pass, as they did for my client, little by little they evolved, and she felt the change of her emotional seasons from a cold winter to a renewed spring.

Victor Frankl, a Holocaust survivor, said, **"When we are no longer able to change a situation, we are challenged to change ourselves."** I have the pleasure of witnessing these changes in my practice on a weekly basis. It may look like anything from a woman who is in an abusive relationship and finally realizes that her spouse will not change: therefore, she must leave the marriage. Or when I work with children who are lost in toxic friendships and finally wake up to the reality that their friend will not change; therefore, they have to leave the friendship. It could be anything from quitting your job, leaving your marriage, or rearranging the furniture in your house. When a situation does not change, hopefully in time, you will wake up that it is you that needs to change. It is these action steps that will subsequently transform your life.

It has been three years since my father died, and, in the beginning, I had never felt more lost without the compass of my father to help me feel the ground beneath me. But by not running away from my feelings, listening to my body, and trusting that my grief wouldn't last forever, my perspective transformed from feeling lost to feeling found. What I ultimately uncovered is that when I am lost the best way to find my way out is not through my father's compass but through my own.

LOST

LISTEN: When you feel lost go to your heart, and ask yourself, "Where in my life am I lost, and what should I do now?"

Sit for 10 minutes with your eyes closed, and listen deeply to your heart for your truest answers. What did you hear?

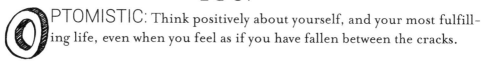

L**O**ST

OPTOMISTIC: Think positively about yourself, and your most fulfilling life, even when you feel as if you have fallen between the cracks.

Notice the difference in your week when you stay optimistic versus pessimistic. What are some positive thoughts you can say to yourself this week?

LO**S**T

SEARCH: When you feel lost, and alone, seek out things that are grounding. This may be saying a prayer, talking to a mentor, or listening to music.

Ask yourself, "What needs to happen in my day to discover more of my life?" Draw one or two pictures of things that help you feel grounded when you feel alone. Use color, this way it won't feel so scary to be lost.

LOS T

TRUST: Trust your intuition. Your intuition is that little voice that is your deepest truth.

When you feel misplaced ask yourself, "What can I do today to feel grounded? What can I trust in my life to feel secure when I feel astray?"

We lose our feathers to grow new ones, we shed our plumage to transform, we need to be lost to be reborn. MJC

26   Be Lost

Be Heard

Your time is limited, so don't waste it living someone else's life. Don't be trapped by dogma – which is living with the results of other people's thinking. Don't let the noise of others' opinions drown out your own inner voice. And most important, have the courage to follow your heart and intuition.
~Steve Jobs

I sit with clients on a daily basis who struggle with speaking their truth. They don't want to disrupt the peace in their work environment, cause any waves with their families, or change their comfortable lifestyle. They would rather sit uncomfortably with the voices that they hear than speak up about how they feel.

When do you hear that **voice**, that authentic voice that sometimes comes as a gentle whisper and at other moments a roaring scream? That voice that you don't always want to listen to because it means you need to face some of your demons in order to get closer to your truth. That voice that also lets you know when you are in the right place at the right time. It is this voice that Michael Meade, author and mythologist, calls your **"inner genius."** Michael talks about inner genius as, "part of the essence of a person; it is the spirit that is already there, hidden inside when a person is born. It can be denied, but cannot simply disappear. Everyone wants to be seen as special because at the level of inner genius everyone is special. Each has some gift to give and each has a unique way of delivering it." By hearing and speaking your inner genius, your spirit will be fed and your whole essence will come alive.

These promptings propel one to reach higher, dig deeper, and not settle for anything less than pure inner authenticity. But gosh darn it if this isn't one of the hardest things to do. Why? Because to do so you need to become honest about how to overcome fear, self doubt, and insecurity. You have to investigate why your fears inhibit you from say, speaking up about your beliefs at a dinner party, belting out your favorite song at karaoke, or communicating your needs to your spouse. It is only when you break free from your fears of speaking your opinions, your truth, that you can begin to live your inner genius.

And why is this vital for personal growth? Because until you start speaking your truth and being heard for who you are, you will struggle with feeling fully alive and whole and have a harder time embracing that you are someone who is significant and deserves respect. It is about believing you are worthy and your voice matters.

There are three ways to help your voice come alive. The first is developing what Carl Jung calls the archetype of the Higher Self. The second is exploring the role "your teachers," those people who trigger your deepest wounds, play in your life. The last is examining how your culture, upbringing and community have shaped your fears and confidence.

I first learned about the archetype of the Higher Self in graduate school, at Pacifica Graduate Institute in Santa Barbara. Our curriculum was based on the teachings of psychoanalyst Carl Jung. Jung believed that the Higher Self is the blueprint for all of humanity, for each individual, it's our ultimate masterpiece. It is the process of unifying all parts of ourselves, the happy and sad, the generous and selfish, the confident and jealous, in order to become more whole. When you become whole you live in a place of more acceptance and less shame. And it is in this space that you discover the beauty of listening to your positive inner voice, the one that says: "You are enough, you deserve to be heard," versus the outer negative voices that say, "Shut up, you need to be more quiet and subdued." It is about silencing those negative voices so you are able to live in your Higher Self, acting from the heart versus the head. Jung states, **"Your visions will become clear only when you can look into your own heart. Who looks outside, dreams; who looks inside, awakes."** When you are able to awaken, you are no longer afraid to speak up.

Discovering your Higher Self began when you were young and you start to separate from your family, propelling you into the individuation process. During this time, you start to discover your authentic personality, your likes and dislikes, everything from how you feel about God to what your favorite color is. Yet, so often this process is muddled by family's religious or cultural beliefs, these belief systems that contaminate who you are meant to be, inhibiting your authentic psyche and, therefore, your Higher Self from developing fully.

Depending on your family and how much control they had over your individuation process is also part of what controls how and when you are free to speak up. Hopefully, once your ego is able to differentiate, you can begin to integrate all sides of your personality and fully come into the Higher Self. When you relax into the Higher Self you will begin to discover your individual divinity and not be silent anymore, because now when you speak it will be birthed from your authentic self not your family or cultures. You will have an engrained belief system that says, "You have every right to be heard." As Carl Jung said, **"The privilege of a lifetime is to become who you truly are."**

Another way to discover your authentic voice is through what I call "your teachers." These are people in your life who may come disguised as your enemies, but if you look deeper, they are really your greatest teachers. They are teaching you to face your fears and find your voice. For example, an acquaintance may treat you in the same painful manner as your mother does, or a boss may intimidate you like your father. These situations trigger your past and give you the opportunity to say the things you were unable to say to your parents when you were a child because you were too young and scared. So often children feel as if their voice was not worthy, that it would not be accepted, or that their opinion would get them in trouble. This process is not about expecting your teachers to say the right thing to make you feel better, it is about you, standing up for yourself. Speaking your truth, regardless of how they react, is what heals the soul. Becoming aware of "your teachers" may be challenging, but if you are willing to look at how they are helping you grow this will launch you to become who you are meant to be.

Lastly, take a look at the times when you wanted to express your opinion or had something that you felt was important to say, and you didn't. You stayed quiet, you were the good little girl or boy who doesn't disrupt the peace. Perhaps this is because you still feel ruled by your family's or society's disapproving message that, "We don't talk about those things" or "That is not appropriate," so you remain silent. This thought process is up to you to change. It is up to you to wake up, crack apart your old rules for when to speak up or stay silent and have the confidence that when you want to share your opinion you do! You shift this fearful mindset by recognizing that your words, and beliefs are just as important, if not more important, than the opinions of your family or culture. They are more significant because they are for you; remember, it is your life you are living.

A rewarding moment in my work is when I am able to witness one of my clients show their true colors to their parents. In one session, I witnessed an adolescent client share with her mother that she felt like she was "walking on eggshells" when she was home because of the dysfunctions she witnessed in her parent's marriage. It was not what she said, but that she believed her voice was important and had enough self-respect to speak her truth. This is what it ultimately comes down to: not whether your speak up or stay quiet, but that you believe you are worthy enough to express your opinion, your words are significant enough to be spoken, and your voice is not controlled by fear or intimidation. You are not afraid anymore: my client was not afraid anymore.

This transformation can be messy and feel like your belief systems are cracking apart, but it is essential to do this work if you want to be heard. Speaking your truth will validate who you are and why you were put on this planet. These feelings will begin to seep into your cells and give you a sense of cellular memory so that next time you want to strap a muzzle over your mouth out of fear or shame, you will instead decide to say, in the words of Katy Perry, **"You're gonna hear me roar."**

VOICE

VIRTUE: Tell the truth, even if it is uncomfortable and fear surrounds you. By telling the truth you will live more in your authentic voice.

My Dad use to tell me, "Molly all you ever owe anyone is the truth. "When do you silence your authentic voice? What would you do differently today? Tell me one of your truths right now.

VICE

OPEN: Open yourself up to hear and follow the promptings of your inner genius.

Use colorful markers, and draw about what in your life you are afraid to listen to. What could you do today to face your fears, in order to discover more of your authentic voice?

VO**i**CE

iNVITE: Invite simplicity into your life; less stuff, fewer obligations, and more space. These actions are clearing your plate so that you have more quiet, and peace in your life.

When you simplify your life you are able to see, and hear more authentically. How can you simplify your life?

VOICE

COURAGE: Raise your hand to speak when shame wants to silence you. This week I want you to speak up about an opinion, or injustice that you feel strongly about.

What would you say if you thought nobody would judge you?

VOICE

EAR: Before I speak, I listen deeply. I ask myself, "What is important about what I am about to say?" Learn discernment between when to speak, and when to listen.

Try practicing listening to your inner voice in order to speak more of your truth. What do you hear when you listen to your truth?

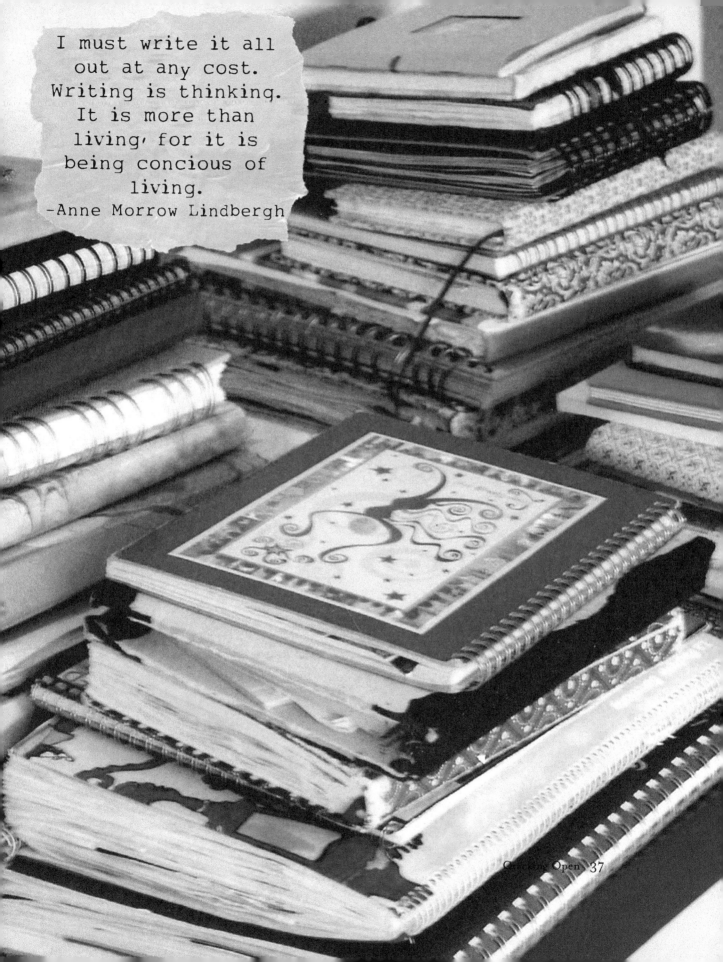

I must write it all
out at any cost.
Writing is thinking.
It is more than
living, for it is
being concious of
living.
-Anne Morrow Lindbergh

Be Seen

Be Seen

"One of the deepest longings of the human soul is to be seen."
~John O' Donohue

The biggest loss from the death of my father is that when I was around him I felt fully seen. He loved all my crazy ideas and bragged to friends and family about my adventures around the world. He laughed at my quirky jokes and when he would hold or hug me it felt as if the world was going to be all-okay. No words even needed to be exchanged, and I knew he saw me and loved me wholeheartedly, and because of this love I was able to show up as me.

What cracks and vulnerabilities in your life do you allow to open so that people can truly see your light and dark and who you really are? I am talking about the beautiful, the ugly, and the ugly that is beautiful. I am talking about letting someone in to see not only when you win the award or receive a promotion at your job, but also when you have to file for bankruptcy or you discovered your spouse is having an affair. I am talking about the moments when you want to be the person who is the "life of the party," but instead you're the person who "falls apart" at the party. Are you okay with all sides of yourself being seen, including your cellulite, sadness, and successes?

Why is it even important to be seen?

It boils down to the fact that people want their lives to be witnessed; otherwise, it feels as if we don't exist. It is about people knowing who you are inside and out which helps us to live wholeheartedly. Although being seen by others is important, we must take care to not look to others for validation and acceptance. It is about being okay with others fully seeing you that is most important.

Why don't we have the courage to allow the world to fully see us? I believe it ultimately comes down to fear and shame. The fear is that we will not be fully loved for who we are and the shame lurks around the parts of ourselves that we don't love or accept. It is very difficult for us to stop asking, "If I don't love this or that about myself, why would others love me?" It is this unconscious mantra that keeps us paralyzed and from exposing the vulnerable sides of ourselves. Often, the only time we let our guard down to be vulnerable is during a crisis or tragedy, and only then because we have to.

When my father passed away, I resisted reaching out to friends and family for support. I would think, "I don't want to bother my friends. Everyone is so busy they don't want to hear about my grief again." This thought process only kept me hiding in pain, and alone, and boy, did I ever feel alone. I did not want the world to see my shadow, my dark sides. In my years as an educator and therapist, I've seen time and time again how hard it is to let others see our shadows. These are the darker parts of ourselves that we don't want to look at or own — jealousy, rage, or insecurity. The issue of hiding our shadow is that when we only allow the world to witness part of our personality, it is impossible to be fully seen.

But to be fully seen you must look at your shadow side. One of the fears I often hear from people is that by starting to look at yourself internally, confronting your demons, you open up a "can of worms" that will lead to a non-stop flow of the dark sides of ourselves. The ironic thing is worms thrive in dampness and darkness and shrivel in the sunlight. This fearful thinking is the number one reason the shadow has so much power.

So what do you do with these fears?

When these uncomfortable emotions arise we need to look at them, expose them to light, embrace the pain, and let the voices of wisdom teach us how to live wholeheartedly. If we cannot embrace all of our sides, the dark and the light, how can we expect anyone else to embrace their dark and light? To be seen, you must not run away; you must stay in the moment and breathe through the uncomfortable feeling.

So, let's start embracing our flaws and looking deeper into our shadow side. First, ask yourself what are some parts of your personality you don't accept, and how often do they play out in your life? Do you compare your life to your family and friends out of insecurity or jealousy, or does your resentment and anger come out in passive-aggressive statements? Do you find yourself playing the victim? Just by taking a few minutes to examine your shadows, do they have less power and do you feel more at peace? Do you feel like you are hiding less and you can see more of yourself?

Next, learn to know the difference between how it feels to be really seen versus how it feels when you're playing a role of what you want the world believe who you are. Observe when you don't tell the truth because you are afraid that someone will not accept you, or you boast or brag to fill the spaces around fear of not being enough. Do you find yourself playing unauthentic roles, such as the perfect mother or father, the unflawed employee, or human being with no failures to be seen? By discovering these differences, not only will you be witnessed in all your glory, but, most importantly, you will feel more freedom from searching for external validation and focus more on your own internal acceptance.

When we expose some of the darker parts of ourselves and come out the other side of that process of introspection, we are more accepting of our flaws. And when we start to accept our flaws, we have so much more fun in life. We start to cultivate compassion for our everlasting spirit and ourselves. Jungian analysts call this becoming "whole." You begin the process of moving from what Jungians call the "undiscovered self" to the "higher integrated self." And when we integrate all part of ourselves, we are no longer hiding anything. When you are able to have an integrated self, you live authentically in the heart versus living in fear in the head. I love the quote by Helen Keller, "The most beautiful things in the world cannot be seen or even touched, they must be felt with the heart."

Please, I beg of you, stop hiding in your fear and shame, let it all hang out, live in the heart like a child — uninhibited and unafraid. Let your awards and failures, your body and soul be exposed for the world to see and with it all out there, you won't live in fear of the "What if they find out about this or that" syndrome. You will just be you, not having to prove anything to anybody except yourself. As sociologist and author Brene Brown says so eloquently, "Courage starts with showing up and letting ourselves be seen." We all yearn to connect. You are not alone. You are in a tribe of beings who want to be witnessed and believed in and to find the courage to ultimately see themselves wholeheartedly. In living this way, you are able to believe with total confidence how important it is to be seen, but even more imperative to believe that it is not that others see me but that I see myself with love and acceptance.

SEEN

SECRET: Don't live in secret anymore. To fully embrace yourself, and allow others to see you, you must come out of the closet and be seen, secrets and all.

Get out your paints, crayons, or markers and draw a picture involving a secret that you have been holding.

sEEN

EXPOSE: This week share one thing about yourself that you have been fearful about exposing. This could be telling your partner that he or she hurt your feelings, to sharing with a friend one of your passions or talents.

What comes up for you when you think about exposing a part of yourself?

seEn

EXPERT: Become an expert of your life. Be willing to go deeper into your emotional world in order to know yourself better.

Tell me what emotions come up for you when I suggest getting to know yourself on a deeper level.

SEE**N**

NOTICE: Notice when you allow people to see you, and when you hide.

What in your life are you most fearful of, and how is that fear inhibiting you from being seen? Doodle the names of the people in your life that you allow to fully see you? And why?

I close my eyes in order to see.
    -Gaugain

Be Dark

Be Dark

"The acceptance of oneself is the essence of the whole moral problem and the epitome of a whole outlook on life."
~C.G. Jung

As children, we are naturally afraid of the dark. We are told this is where the boogie man lives. The image of this scary man that could hurt you was implanted in many of our brains. Even at 43, my heart still beats fast when I am in my house alone and it's dark. I don't know where to step or if something around the corner is going to jump out at me. The dark often represents fear, pain, or the unknown, but, if embraced, it can often be a monumental step towards happiness.

What I want to talk about in this chapter is emotional darkness, or anxiety and depression. Anxiety disorders are the most common mental illness in the United States, and women experience depressive disorders twice as frequently as men. After twenty years of working with families and children, I know that anxiety and depression do not just affect a selected few, they are common afflictions. We all feel these emotions, but in different ways.

Some of us may feel either or both of them so deeply that we need medication. Others may just feel low or nervous once in a while. Anxiety may present itself in your life as a manically racing heart, or you may deal with it by running around, staying busy with daily tasks in order to not feel lonely or lost. While depression may feel as if a dark cloud has entered your body, creating a dragging weight of sadness, or as if you just fell in black well of deep despair, gripped with fear and hopelessness. These emotions may cause you to question your decisions, your purpose or value in life, and prevent you from experiencing happiness or joy.

Even though anxiety and depression are two separate diagnoses, they are often experienced simultaneously. If you feel anxious one day, you will often feel depressed as well. They both come in one pretty package. And with this package comes the pattern of masking these challenging emotions with food, sex, drugs, or alcohol. You may reach for any numbing agent to chase away the pounding heart or to cast aside the dark blanket that is covering your spirit.

And on top of already feeling hopeless, there is an unspoken sentiment that you can just "pull up your boot straps and get on with it." Well, as many of my clients who deal with these issues have said, "If that is all it took to move on, I would do it every second of every day." The truth is that to pull yourself out of these emotions often feels like climbing Mount Everest.

So what do you do?

I do not mean to speak simplistically about mental illnesses that affect 40 million people, and I encourage you to seek professional medical treatment as necessary, but I have discovered two useful tools that may help you feel more grounded when the demons strike. They are to speak and to listen.

Speaking to someone and getting support can make a big difference. I don't care if you tell a teacher, preacher, therapist, or friend, but tell your story; it will help you feel much less isolated and alone. When did you first start to feel anxiety or depression enter your life? How does it affect your life today? What things do you do to help you feel more free? Don't feel ashamed to reach out and lean on others for support and healing.

The second piece of advice is, as Shakespeare spoke so wisely, **"Darkness has its uses."** Do not lock these dark emotions away in a closet, ignoring their voices and expecting them to go away, because, like mold, they will just grow. If you had diabetes, you would not just ignore its symptoms. No, you would take time in your day to take your insulin and watch your diet so that you can live a healthier life. Anxiety and depression are the same. Take time everyday to attend to its voices by writing, doing yoga, meditating, and walking, integrating these tools into your life will help support you when you feel dark. Instead of hating your anxiety or depression, listen to it and find a way to meld it into your life. You may find that it is your anxiety and depression that have led you to be a more creative artist, an empathetic therapist, or compassionate mother. If you open up to its wisdom, you may find that this darkness is one of your greatest teachers.

Deepak Chopra says it beautifully, "It is considered impossible to untangle the complexities of emotions, and even if one succeeded for a brief time (miraculously) to tame anger, fear, worry, jealousy, and insecurity, new emotions would spring up, or a deeper layer of the old issues would surface. Learning to center yourself, to see your emotions as productive rather than your enemy, and dealing with negative emotions as objectively as possible are all good steps of progress."

I did not realize that I had anxiety until I was an adult. I just accepted being teased as a child with nicknames like "gremlin." I always thought I just had a lot of energy. As an adult, this energy manifested itself in a hyper-busyness. Friends would tease me that by 8 a.m. I would have already hiked a mountain, cleaned the house, and baked a cake. This may be true, but what they didn't know was that doing all these chores was a mechanism to chase away the dark feelings of anxiety. I would stay busy so I wouldn't have to face the demons inside my soul. Then my first child was born, and the demons came screaming, resulting in a terrible case of post-partum depression.

I was so tired recovering from childbirth and then being up all night breastfeeding, that I just felt miserable. I felt robbed for being a woman, the procreator. I would envy other women and men and their ability to wake up in the morning, drink their coffee, and go to the office, while I sat on the couch nursing and watching *The View*. I felt like I was in a bubble of baby misery.

During those dark days it was ugly. I did not want to be a mother. And the heartbreaking shame of that feeling created a constant abysmal feeling of being inside a dark cloud of loneliness. It was so incredibly painful to be around other mothers who were experiencing the joy of their newborn children. I not only felt separate from other mothers, but disconnected from my own sweet newborn as well. To say that these times were cracking me open was an understatement. I felt as if the whole world was cracking apart and I was falling in.

But I climbed out, and so can you.

By engaging in daily rituals of walking, journaling, and speaking with trusted friends about its hold upon me, these demons had less of a grip upon my soul. I also began to listen and hear what I needed at each moment: "Molly, call your therapist for some support, take a nap, go for a run," knowing that if I stopped listening I would be overcome with its power. I now know more, have confronted more, and am more honest with myself about my anxiety and postpartum depression. By looking at the roots of my postpartum depression I was able to give it a voice. We all feel the confusing emotions around depression, anxiety, rage, jealousy, or grief. We all struggle. All I can say is: let it be, let it have its days, and get support around the emotions. And again, please talk to a friend, family member, therapist, acupuncturist, healer, priest, pastor, whoever will listen. But don't stay quiet. The voice in your head that says, "I am a mess and no one wants to hear about my problems" must be quieted. This mantra will only feed the misery.

Begin by telling your story to me in the pages ahead, and I promise you will transform in one way or another. We therapists call this storytelling "narrative healing." Every time you tell your story, you take away its power. So let's pull down the veils and open the curtains, in order to take away the power and face that dark boogie man head on.

Dark

ETERMINATION: Be determined not to let your dark side be locked away in a closet anymore. Don't hide your dark thoughts and let them fester.

Share here how anxiety or depression has touched your life? What do your anxious or depressed moments look like?

DARK

ATTACHMENT: Try not to get so attached to your dark moments. Remind yourself time, and time again, to breathe. Trust that these dark emotions will pass, and another moment, emotion, and day will come.

Write down a dark emotion that you are attached to right now, and then write down the opposite emotion. How do both emotions make you feel?

DA**R**K

REALITY: One of the greatest shifts I see in my clients is when they can look at their reality with objectivity. Not allowing the stories they have told themselves for years, be their truth.

Today, tell yourself one truth about your life that you have been keeping in the dark, out of fear or shame. What patterns of behavior have you created, to either cover up, or get through your days of darkness?

DAR**K**

KINDNESS: There is no way you will survive your dark side unless you wrap your soul in kindness blanket.

When you are able to cultivate self-compassion for yourself, you are then able to have deep kindness for all those around you. What is one kind thing you can say to yourself when your dark feelings arise?

EVERYBODY

Our life is the creation of our mind.

THE BUDDHA

The quieter you become,
the more you hear. Ram Dass

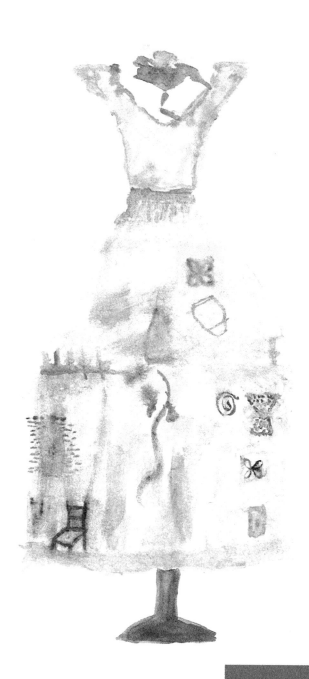

MtR

Be Friended

"If you live to be a hundred, I want to live to be a hundred minus one day so I never have to live without you."
~A.A. Miline, Winnie-the-Pooh

One of my most touching moments of friendship happened shortly after my father died. I was dropping my daughter off at a play date with some other children and one of the other mothers, a friend, said, "Molly I have something for you." She pulled out the most beautiful painting of a man and a tree. She knew I loved trees and explained that while she was in New York City with her husband, they saw this painting and it just reminded her of my father and me. I broke into tears. It was one of the most thoughtful gestures I have ever received.

Friendships are the mirrors into our souls.

Friends offer the gift of showing us how to live, love, and laugh. There is an immense amount of comfort in a friend's voice when you are feeling sad, or support in the grasp of their hand when you are feeling weak. There is nothing better than a deep belly laugh with a dear friend. We were put onto this planet to be in community with one another, and friendship is one of the purest ways to feel this connection. This profound love is a catalyst for growth for the body, mind, and spirit.

Strong friendships help you feel less stress, lower blood pressure, reduce the risk of anxiety or depression, and promote brain health. Friendships have a stronger effect on our psychological well-being than even family relationships. In a study at Harvard, they discovered that women with no friends are four times more likely to die from breast cancer than those women with a friendship network. That's a startling statistic, but no question, battling illness, taking on a challenge, starting a new job, or entering into a new phase of life is much easier with the support of a friend.

When I am working with my clients, it is very important to find out how they have survived loss, abuse, or tragedy in their lives. Nine out of ten times they will answer that a friend made a difference, got them through the moments when they did not think they could survive. These friends called when they needed to hear a voice, dropped off soup to feed their family when it felt impossible to cook, or provided a safe space for them to cry without embarrassment or shame.

This being said, friendships are not always about laughter, love, and support. Sometimes, like any relationship, they can turn or be toxic and dampen your spirit. Look closely at the people with whom you surround yourself and how they are a reflection of your own soul. Who fills you up, makes you feel more authentic, whole and alive, and who steals your soul and your energy, making you feel depleted, judged, or ugly inside and out?

Brene Brown spoke of this concept of friendship at a workshop I attended at the Omega Institute in upstate New York. Her daughter came home from school upset after being teased by some classmates. This led them into a beautiful discussion about "the marble jar" of friendship. When friends do kind things for you, ask you about your ailing parents, or are able to apologize for saying or doing something unkind, they get a marble in the jar of friendship. And conversely, if friends are not kind, tease you, gossip about you or do not stand for the same values as you do, they don't get a marble. If you have friendships where the marble job is empty, that may be a toxic friendship.

How do you know if you're in a toxic friendship? First, pay attention to your body. Does your stomach feel uneasy and your head hurt after talking to or hanging out with a certain friend? Trust these feelings. Our cells have memory, and if you have awareness around how your body feels when you are in a toxic situation or conversation, it will remind you to not spend time with these people. Then with a recipe of strength, courage, and just plain ole determination, you can stop making an effort and feeding its toxicity. Hopefully, what will follow is clarity about what direction the friendship should go. You may need to build up the courage, strength, and heart armor to slowly pull away. You may live in a big city where it's easy to avoid these friends, but if you live in a small town where you run into people quite often, or have overlapping social circles, you can't just disappear, you need to find a way to be in the same physical space with these people, but mentally distance yourself.

How can you do this?

Before you know you will be in the presence of those people who might trigger bad feelings, check in with your inner voice and trust its wisdom. Ask yourself, "Should I go tonight? Is it worth feeling crummy, or can I go and have a good time?" Listen to the answer. If it's "no," you may wish to stay home and take a bath, have a cup of tea, be with your family, or enjoy your own company. And if you hear a "yes," go, but take some time before you enter the room to surround yourself with a bubble of love, light, and levity to protect you from feeling sad or hurt. Most importantly, if you arrive somewhere and do not feel authentic or are not having a good time, go home. It is these actions and decisions, and the boundaries they establish that will allow you to deal with these relationships in a much more positive way.

The *New York Times* published an article on this topic saying, "Psychologists consider it an inevitable life stage, a point where people achieve enough maturity and self-awareness to know who they are and what they want out of their remaining years, and have a degree of clarity about which friends deserve full attention and which are a drain."

These moments are eye-opening and challenging because it is not just about building boundaries or giving a friendship less attention, it is also about having the awareness and heart to ask yourself, **"What part do I play in this unhealthy relationship?** How is this toxic relationship serving me?" Quite often these difficult relationships are formed because you bond with this other person over your traumas, insecurities, and past wounds. Caroline Myss author and psychologist coined this action, "woundology."

"Woundology" revolves around connecting with another person by participating in negative behaviors, such as gossip, in order to connect. Generally in these friendships you are defining yourself by your physical, emotional, or social wounds, not by your authentic self. Not only are these relationships unhealthy, they keep you in the victim role and inhibit you from healing from your past wounds. The key to change is to become aware of when you are in a friendship that revolves around your wounds and not around your Higher Self. By staying in these relationships you are keeping yourself from having more authentic and healthy friendships. Let your friendships not revolve around your wounds, but surround you with love so that you have a place to heal your wounds.

I was looking at a beautiful woven antique quilt the other day, and it made me think of my friendships. Each quilt piece reminded me how relationships can be complicated and intricate, that they take time to create and bring comfort, warmth, and beauty. As with healthy friendships, this quilt is always something I can grab to keep me safe and warm in this beautiful and sometimes challenging world. It reminded me of a favorite quote from Rumi: **"Be with those who help your being."** Be with friends who don't have an agenda and are with you because they want to love and support you. Be with friends who can laugh about your idiosyncrasies with and celebrate your successes without jealousy or competition. Be with friends who can have your grieving heart with them, even when they are on a trip with their husband to New York City.

FRIEND

FLIP. I have a phrase that I say when I am struggling with a friend. It is "flip the coin." If you are feeling negatively about a friend, "flip the coin" and try to be in a space of positivity.

I know this is not easy, but notice the difference you feel when you have thoughts of compassion versus anger with your friend. Draw two coins. On one coin write your thoughts of frustration around a friendship. Now draw a second coin, and write your thoughts around why you care for this friendship. Notice the difference you feel between the two coins.

FRIEND

RADIANT: Spend time around people who make you feel radiant and alive.

Tell me about how your friendships make you feel radiant. Spend time this week with one person who brings out your light, and also makes you feel safe in your dark.

FRIEND

INTIMATE: Be vulnerable in your friendships, and do not be afraid to share your stories, sadness, or soul.

Reach out this week to one friend, and spend in an intimate moment with them. This may look like sharing a vulnerable story, or creating a fun night for the two of you.

FRIEND

ESSENCE: Remember your true essence. Do not change who you are for what you feel other people want you to be.

Tell me about a time when you changed your personality for a friend, and how that made you feel.

FRIEND

NEED: We all need friends in order to feel whole. This connection is just as important as eating and drinking.

Why do you need friends in your life? How do they fulfill you up?

FRIEN

DEVOTION: Be as devoted to your friendships. Remember what you give out to others, you will receive back tenfold.

Make sure someone is filling up his or her "friendship marble jar" because of you. How have you been devoted to your friendships?

"Your spirit is mingled with mine that what touches you, touches me." Rumi

Be Brave

"I learned that courage was not the absence of fear, but the triumph over it. The brave man is not he who does not feel afraid, but he who conquer that fear."
~Nelson Mandela

There are moments in our lives, on just about a daily basis, when we feel that stirring in our belly or tightness in the chest or maybe even a fluttering in our hearts, when we have come face to face with one of our fears, and need to be brave. These moments may push you out of your comfort zone, and look like interviewing for a job that may feel out of your league, going on a blind date when you are not feeling so attractive, or getting on your bike to ride miles upon miles for AIDS when all you really want to do is melt your body into the couch and watch reality TV.

This is about saying "yes" to an adventure even if your fears are saying "no."

This is about cracking open to see how brave you can really be in this lifetime. When you are presented with these opportunities, you may hear the negative voices: "What am I thinking, I could never get that job, that man or woman would never be attracted to me, or I am not in good enough physical condition to ride to the next block." Instead of listening to the voice of defeat, delve deeper and ask your heart, "Should I do this?" Nine out of ten times you will hear the answer "Yes." You can counter the negative thoughts with positive ones. "I have always wanted to try something new in my career, or I am enjoyable and interesting person anyone would be lucky to spend an evening with me, or I want to test my physical strength." Or just repeat the quote by Eleanor Roosevelt, **"You must do the thing you think you cannot do."**

When we think about being brave, most people think about feats of physical bravery: Diana Nyad stumbling onto the beach after swimming 110 miles or Sir Edmond Hillary summiting Mount Everest. There is an amazing emotional transformation when we have the bravery to aspire to physical transformation. When we move the body physically, we release a lot of our negative emotional toxins to make room for more light and love. We create more endorphins, which in turn creates more happiness. Physical activity improves self-confidence, alleviates anxiety, and boosts creativity. But what I have realized, in my years as a therapist, is that sometimes emotional bravery, the courage to confront a family member after they hurt your feelings, or standing up for a cause when it is not popular, can be even harder than physical bravery.

When it comes to emotional bravery, it takes just as much work and effort. Jack Kornfeld has shared his story about how he became a Buddhist monk. He had a tumultuous childhood and recognized there was not a lot of support in the West for his feelings of fear and anger, so he went to the East to learn how to deal with these emotions. It was in the East he was able to slow down and be in a culture that values focusing on painful emotions. Because of this environment, he learned how important it is to spend time learning how to be emotionally brave. Being emotionally brave allows you to embrace your feelings knowing that they have a significant place in this world. When you understand that your emotions are valid and necessary, you also understand you are valid as a human being as well. It is about recognizing that you have every right to feel and experience every emotion without shame or guilt.

At times it can be hard to be emotionally brave because we are not always taught about how to work with these feelings when they arise. As discussed, we are encouraged to "pull up our boot straps" or "stop crying and get over it." However, my advice to you is to look at the shame around your emotions that create spoken and unspoken messages that inhibit you from being brave and cause you to stuff them deep down inside your body until you either get sick or are on the brink of a mental breakdown. The key is to counteract this shame with self-compassion and begin to stop and pay attention to how your difficult feelings are affecting your emotional and physical well being.

Here is an exercise that will strengthen who you are in order to create more bravery. Let's say someone, a co-worker, friend, family, or spouse, says something hurtful or degrading to you. I want you to write down what emotions came up for you in that moment: was it anger, frustration, or confusion? Then go one layer deeper into the root of the emotion. Ask yourself how you felt when you were degraded as a child by your parents, peers, or teachers? Then go one more layer deeper. When you felt these emotions, what story would you tell yourself? Was it something like, "I am useless, unworthy, not important?" By going deeper into your emotions, you find out the core of the negative story you tell yourself, and then you can begin to un-attach and tell yourself a new story.

This exercise is what I call, "healing the emotional child." You, as an adult, self-talk to your 7, 37 or 87-year old self the way you wish someone would have talked to you growing up. Tell yourself, **"Even in your dark mo-**

ments, you are a beautiful, intelligent, and loving human being. You have so many gifts to give to the world. I accept all of you." This is one tool to help you when you are not feeling very emotionally brave. Knowing that practice helps develop a skill, practice strengthening your emotional bravery.

It is these physical and emotional benefits of bravery that feed the soul more than any big house, fancy car, or designer clothes. So what is stopping you? Fear, failure, or falling on your face? Be brave enough to not let those "F's" stand in the way of living a life of courage. Cheryl Strayed speaks of this in her memoir, *Wild*. **"You will learn a lot about yourself if you stretch in the direction of goodness, of bigness, of kindness, of forgiveness, of emotional bravery. Be a warrior for love."** Be a warrior of love for the self, love that you can hike any mountain, attain any job, go on any date, face any fear, and come out a braver human being. So be an emotional and physical warrior, stand tall, take chances and do not let fear stop you from your truest self. The benefits will always outweigh your fears.

BRAVE

BOLD: In order to be brave, you have to be bold. Boldly jump off the cliff of vulnerability to strengthen your emotional bravery.

This month try one new physical, and one new emotional feat. Share with me how you are physically and emotionally bold in your life.

BAVE

ESPONSIBILITY: It is your responsibility to strengthen your bravery muscle. No one will do it for you.

Think of a marathon—it is the runner that actually has to run the 26 miles. They will have water and food support systems, but it is the runner who has to do the work. This applies to both emotional and physical bravery.

Paint or draw three things you can do to become more physically and emotionally bravery.

BR**A**VE

ATTACHMENT: We can become to attached to our patterns of behaviors, and actually convince ourselves that we don't need to change.

Believing that you can stay the same from 4 to 104-years old is only holding you back from living. Begin to detach yourself, or as I call it "cut the umbilical cord" to behaviors that do not serve you anymore, and begin to feel more free.

Look at your attachments and patterns of behavior that hold you back from being brave. Tell me how you can change one behavior, or pattern, this week leaving your comfort zone.

BRA**V**E

VALIDATE: Allow yourself to receive validation for being brave.

This week, when someone gives you a compliment, stop, let it seep into your cells, and say thank you. Share on this page a compliment that you received, and why you believe it is still with you today.

BRAVE

ENERGY: By attending to your physical and emotional bravery, you will feel energized.

Notice the difference in your body when you do something physical. Do you feel more alive, secure, and confidant? Notice the difference in your body when you allow yourself to be vulnerable with a friend, family member, or foe. Do you feel a bit lighter, stronger, and proud? How do you want to become more emotionally and physically brave in your life?

"So come to the pond, or the river of your imagination, or the harbor of your longing, and put your lips to the world. And live your life."
Mary Oliver, Red Bird

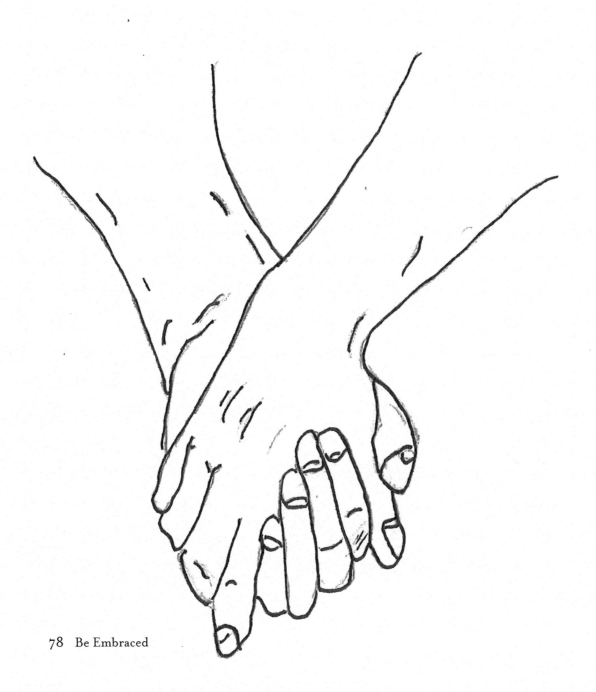

Be Embraced

The heart's memory eliminates the bad and magnifies the good; and thanks to this artifice we manage to endure the burdens of the past. "
~Gabriel García Marquez

I grew up in a big Irish Catholic family in Omaha, Nebraska, so I am not sure if I have learned more about the family system as a therapist or through my family of origin. But one thing I know for sure is that there are few things in life more complex and that have more of an impact on who you are and how you walk in the world than your family. Families shape your outlook, your perspective, and your roles as a daughter, son, sister, brother, mother, or father. Your family can be a powerful influence over so many of your feelings, so why wouldn't you want to find a way to better understand this dynamic?

In fact, it's the very first thing I do with my clients address the hidden secrets of their family system. Those bonds are so tight that most people are afraid to crack their families open and examine them in the light. Yet, it is in this area of exploration where so many answers lie. In my experience, when people feel safe to open up about their family with honesty and courage, shame disappears and transformation happens. In this space of vulnerability, they begin to recognize how their childhood traumas and traditions have created many of their negative behaviors. By becoming aware of their negative emotions and behaviors, they can create change.

My clients often report that they've sought therapy because they are noticing that they are acting out the same dysfunctions with their children that they experienced as children. They don't want to spank, or use passive-aggressive statements to discipline their children. They don't want to drink nightly to relax or numb out to the TV. They want a different story and a different life. By talking honestly about their family, they are able walk in the world with more truth and compassion and decipher what stories are real and what stories they hold onto for protection. Once they make these connections, it's easier to modify their behavior.

So now think about your family and all your issues that you have never shared with a soul. Think about how these issues affect your daily life. And think about why you have fear of sharing these with anyone, even close confidants. Now I am not saying you should take out an ad in the *New York Times* about your family, but I am saying that if you share your story with one person your secrets have less power and you gain more awareness about how they affect your life. By telling your story, fear dissipates and healing occurs.

Starting today, how can you deal with these loving, complex, and at times painful relationships?

There are two ways to do this. The first step is to look at the wounds and traumas you experienced in your family as a child. You may have felt, and still feel, responsible for some of those issues, be they alcoholism, neglect, or abuse. I don't mean to simplify childhood, especially when speaking about abuse, but once you understand those dynamics were not your fault and were completely out of your control, you begin to heal. If you can recognize that you were a child and could not control your situation you can create more compassion and less guilt or shame around your pain.

The second step is best explained by a quote from psychologist James Hillman, "If you are still being hurt by an event that happened to you at twelve, it is the thought that is hurting you now." There comes a time where you have to stop blaming your parents, relatives, or caretakers for your pain and look at your thoughts and how they control your unhappiness. You need to embrace the present moment and ask yourself,

"How can I move forward from today?

How can I start living the life I want to live instead of re-living the wounds from my childhood for so many years?" By stepping out of your childhood story and jumping into your adult life, you be able to embrace more joy.

Regardless of your upbringing or what your family looks like today, it is important to try to accept your family for who they are and for who they are not. This takes time, as your feelings are forever evolving. We often have an image in our heads of an unrealistic family that does not have fights or dysfunctions, that always see eye to eye and never get pissed off at one another. And because of this false image, people are often disappointed in and frustrated with their actual family. The truth is that every family is imperfect, hilarious, nurturing, messy and complicated, but when you can begin to deconstruct your stories with love and compassion and embrace the truth of your family, you can begin to stop your own dysfunctional patterns and lead a healthier life. Simply put, you can begin to move forward instead of moving backwards.

Embracing the truth about your family is not a walk in the park and it may take six months to sixty years, and that is okay. This acceptance does not need to be rushed, but when the time comes that you are able to embrace your family for who they are, it is easier to become more authentic and show them who you are. You cannot expect them to truly know you unless you show them who you are. Until you fully show up, you cannot assume they are unable or unwilling to accept you. So show them your voice, your authentic self, your troubles and tattoos, your opinions and objections. Let them embrace you for your differences and teach them about how change is inevitable and being open-minded is refreshing.

Sit for a moment and just recognize how your body feels when you think about your family from a place of love versus frustration or hate. And, more importantly, think about how your body feels when you accept yourself with love versus hate and acceptance versus change. I believe with time you will be able to embrace your family with more forgiveness and compassion and, subsequently, embrace more of your life. So let's follow the advice of George Bernard Shaw about accepting our families, **"If you cannot get rid of the family skeleton, you may as well make it dance."**

EMBRACE

FFORT: Make the effort to start embracing your family for who they are, not from a place of changing them.

What will it take for you to start the process of embracing your family, warts and all? Write down one thing that you have not embraced about your family and why. Use a crayon or marker; this playfulness may add a little levity.

EMBRACE

MEDITATION: When you are feeling triggered by your family, spend one minute in meditation, surrounding yourself in a bubble of light.

Meditate one time this week, two times next week, and three the following week. Even if it is for three minutes, do your best to sit in silence. Share with me what comes up for you when you think about meditating. Notice the overall difference after you meditate.

EM**B**RACE

BLINDED: Do not be blinded by the denial around your family. The sooner you come to terms with the truth of who they are, and what they are capable of giving you, the more accepting you will be.

How can you step out of the wounds of your childhood and into your adult life? Take off the blindfold, and write down three truths about your family that you have not been able to face.

EMBACE

ESTORE: Often when you spend time with your family you may need some time to restore your body, mind, and spirit.

Write down things that help you feel more restored. This may be taking a bath, going for a run, drinking tea, or just being alone on a walk.

EMBRCE

ACCEPT: In your own time, and in your own way, try to accept your family for who they are, remembering nobody is perfect.

We are all on a growing spectrum, and when we accept our own flaws, with self-compassion, we are more apt to accept our own family's as well. What is one thing you can accept about your family?

EMBRACE

CHANGE: At this moment really let this concept soak in: "You cannot change anyone, you can only change yourself."

What are two or three things you can change about yourself that will help you embrace your family?

EMBRACE

EQUAL: We are all the same, rich or poor, man or woman, short or tall. We all feel emotions: love, loss, and longings. We all need the necessities of life: water, food, and shelter.

When we are able to take each other off the pedestals of perfection, we are able to live on this planet together, more cohesive, and less divided.

What two or three things do you have in common with one of your family members?

discover

Cracking Open 89

Breathing Space

Be Adventurous

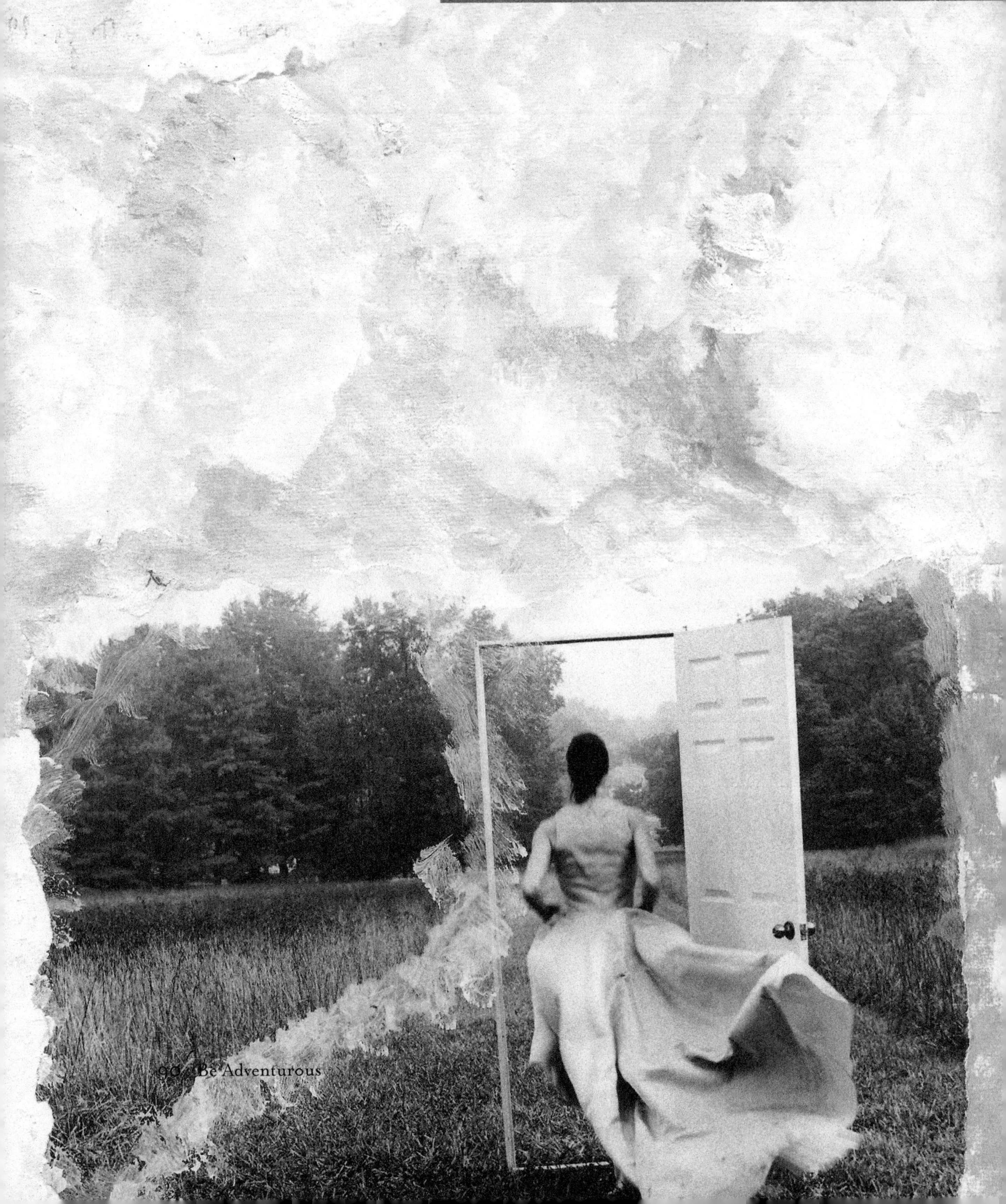

Be Adventurous

"This is love: to fly toward a secret sky, to cause a hundred veils to fall each moment. First to let go of life. Finally, to take a step without feet." ~Rumi

I will never forget the first time I stepped on a plane to fly internationally. My whole body buzzed with euphoria and bliss. I was leaving the Midwest to travel 6,534 miles away. I was 18 years old and had never been further than a three hour car ride to Iowa. I was on a high school trip to the holy lands of Egypt and Israel, and then Italy. Changing planes in New York, I got to see different-colored faces, unique attire, and hear several foreign languages—I thought I had died and gone to heaven. I knew at that moment that travel was my drug of choice—it is any searcher's dream. Now, twenty-one years later, I have traveled all over the United States, throughout Indonesia, Thailand, Cambodia, Vietnam, Italy, France, Germany, Austria, England, Ireland, Chile, Canada, Mexico, and India, as well as lived in Barcelona, Spain. I spent my 20's in Europe, my 30's in Southeast Asia, and my 40's in India. One of the beautiful things about my adventures is that they did not come by way of a high paying salary or a trust fund. They came from a teacher's salary and a financially creative soul. I now trust that when I get the magnetic pull from my gut to go, I go!

When I hear the word "adventure" my mind instantly gravitates towards booking a flight to anywhere from Omaha to Osaka. But being adventurous is not all about air travel; living with a sense of adventure is about cracking open the body, mind, and spirit to receive a new experience. It is about taking yourself out of your comfort zone of life and asking your heart, **"How can I let my soul soar in a way that I have not before? How can I confront my fears so that they do not have such a tight grip upon me? How can I live the fullest life I was meant to live?"** It may involve getting on a plane, walking around the corner to a new café in your neighborhood, taking up a new hobby, trying new foods, or going on a blind date. Being adventurous untethers the soul and allows you to learn about the parts of yourself you have not discovered or maybe did not want to see.

By sitting on a balcony and watching the sunrise from across the globe, hearing the sound of foreign voices, or digesting spices that you did not even know existed, you will transform. By saying yes to a job that scares you or "coming out" in your sexuality to your family and friends or learning to ride a bike, drive a car, or paraglide, you will break free from your imprisoned mind into becoming a more adventurous human being. I would not be who I am today—

less judgmental, more open, able to speak Spanish, and appreciative of our diverse world—if I did not love to "travel" in mind, body, and soul. It is by being adventurous that you are able to open your heart to develop more compassion and an expansive state of being, suspend judgments towards people, places, and predicaments that make you uncomfortable, and wake up to all your senses in order to live a more fulfilling life in the heart versus the head.

When I see a client stuck in a job, relationship, or any other aspect of their life, I encourage them to get in a car, or on a plane, train, or bicycle, and invite adventure into their life. I have a client that was stuck in life and in an unhealthy marriage: living in a world of Range Rovers and fancy houses, her value was dependent on how much money she had in her bank account. She thought adventure meant buying a new Gucci purse. With all this "stuff" came a fear of being alone. I suggested she travel from Bend to Portland, 170 miles, for the day. From this adventure, slowly and with support, she has been able to travel out of a unhealthy marriage, a job that she felt undervalued her, and, most importantly, from having little confidence and superficial values to feeling worthy and finding that life is really about community, her children, and self worth far beyond wealth. It is about believing in yourself more than your fears. It is about looking at your life through a lens of adventure versus fears and superficial images.

So what veils are stopping you?

Yes, money, time, work, and family commitments can be challenges, but don't let them be the reasons you don't break out of your comfort zone once in a while. What is really stopping you is your mind. Don't let fear, rules, or regulations control you from living an adventurous life. Once your mind breaks free, you will be able to fully embrace this one life with an adventurous soul. You will be able to let your wings fly, your heart soar, and your spirit soak in all that this diverse world has to offer. Embrace the wise words of Helen Keller, "Avoiding danger is no safer in the long run than outright exposure. Life is either a daring adventure, or nothing." Being adventurous is about breaking free from the confines of comfort in order to unveil the life you are meant to live. So strip off your veils and remember where there is a will, there is a way and **Oh, the places you will go!**

FLY

F AITH: When you are looking at an adventure, have faith. It is impossible to know what will be in front of you, but learn to trust that if you hear the call of the wild, you should respond.

Write down one adventure that you have taken that was decided solely upon faith. How can you become more adventurous in your daily life?

FLY

LIGHT-HEARTED: When you are on an adventure, whether that be riding your bike to the beach, or trekking across Nepal, your heart beams rays of light.

What boldness needs to happen to create more adventure in your life?

Draw a picture of a heart, and inside put all the emotions you feel when you are on an adventure. Keep this somewhere to remind yourself how important it is to have adventure in your life.

FL **Y**

YOUTHFUL: Adventures allow you to feel younger in your skin, spirit, and soul.

Look back at photos of you when you were traveling. Do you look more relaxed, alive, and youthful? Now ask yourself, where have you always dreamed of going? What's stopping you?

"The big question is whether you are going to be able to say a hearty yes to your adventure."

~Joseph Campbell

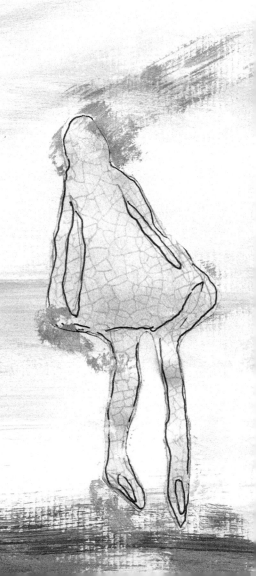

Be Peaceful

Be Peaceful

"We can never obtain peace in the outer world until we make peace with ourselves"
~Dalai Lama XIV

If you asked my close friends and family to describe my personality, I doubt anyone would use the word "peaceful." I am not one who is naturally wired that way. I am someone that has had to work hard to be tranquil, and it sometimes amazes me that I can sit calmly for six to seven hours with my clients just being in the present moment. In this chapter, I would love to share with you my tools and techniques to calm the chaotic mind, or as the Buddhists call it "the monkey mind."

There are three things that have changed my life. They are **deep breathing, yoga, and meditation.** This is my trifecta for peace. By engaging in these three practices, I have learned to let go of my outer world to find more peace in my inner world. As the Buddha said, **"Peace comes from within. Do not seek it without."** So let's go within and let this chapter transform your internal mindset to enhance your external essence.

I remember watching my children breathing when they were newborns. They would take deep inhales and slow exhales. This natural state was connecting them to a deeper level of joy, peace, and relaxation. On the opposite end of the spectrum, I observe so many of my clients breathing heavily and rapidly as if they've just run a marathon. How and when did we lose our slow rhythmic breath and develop short, shallow, rushed breaths? Why does our hectic and chaotic life take over our natural born ability to stop and breathe?

It is because we take our breathing for granted. We breathe all day long, each and every moment, and yet we are largely unconscious of how this act keeps us alive, calms the nervous system, lowers stress, and helps us feel less anxious. It is this oxygen exchange that slows your heartbeat, lowers or stabilizes your blood pressure, enhances concentration, and allows you to tap into one of your body's strongest self-healing mechanisms.

Stop right now and take three deep breaths.

Now after breathing, identify on a scale from 1-10—1 being complete calm and 10 being very anxious—where you are. I am guessing you are now lower than you were when you started reading this chapter. I hope you can see why breathing is so simple, yet so profoundly powerful.

One place where I do more deep breathing than anywhere else is in my yoga classes. It is very rare that I walk out of a yoga class feeling less peaceful than I did walking in. One of the foremost yoga teachers in the world, B.K.S. Iyengar said, **"Yoga teaches us to cure what need not be endured and endure what cannot be cured."** And God knows, we all need a little more curing and a little more enduring.

I took one of my first yoga classes after I had just moved back to the States from Barcelona. I walked in scared and nervous, continually hearing my inner critic shouting, "You can't do this, look at all these yogis, you don't belong here." I ignored these discouraging words, put my mat down towards the back of the room, and began to sit quietly. In this split, second I learned a fundamental life concept; when you are struggling with something, just simply begin the action and observe what follows.

The class was a stew of emotions. I was angry when I couldn't do this or that pose I feared that I looked like a fool when I fell out of tree pose, and was resentful towards the other people in the class. "Oh, they think they are so good." Then the mother of all emotions arose: guilt. I started beating myself up for having any of these feelings. "My God, Molly, you are in a yoga class, can you not be nice even in yoga?" In this moment, I remembered an Anne Lamott quote, **"If you have a body, you are entitled to the full range of feelings. It comes with the package."** Thank you, Anne.

After an hour and a half of struggle, resistance, and also surrender, I was able to lie down in the final pose of *shaivasana*. It is the lying down and doing nothing that allowed me to accept my situation and recognize how being in this space created a lot of emotions, especially an overall a sense of peace.

How come sun salutations, forward folds, backbends, and inversions bring up so many feelings? We humans are prone to hold our "stuff": stuff being our toxic emotions in our body. They are what cause disease, sickness, injuries, and just really bad moods. Yoga is one way we can move these emotions out of the body through stretching and twisting, releasing all the old stories that we have told ourselves for years, leaving space for light, love, joy, and peace to arrive.

Take two minutes right now and begin in *taedasana*, just standing straight up, and offer up an intention, what you want for your day — maybe more peace, joy, or calmness. Then, move your body in whatever way feels natural and end by laying down in a "corpse pose" to rest. In just these few minutes, do you feel more peaceful? Do you feel as if the world is more of a loving place than a place that wants to hurt you? And do you feel healthier in your mind, body, and spirit? I am guessing most of your answers will be yes.

And now the third prong of the trifecta, meditation. To begin meditation, find a space that is quiet. Be seated on a cushion or chair and sit up erect and relaxed. Close your eyes softly and begin with three deep breaths. Let your mind be open and your heart be filled with loving compassion for whatever arises. Meditation is about sitting and being the witness to the body and mind. By sitting quietly and breathing, you are allowing yourself to recognize that you are not your thought patterns. You are of a higher essence of being. And when you are the observer, you find a way to be in a space of awareness versus judgment, creating more solace and peace in your life. It is simple in that you are just sitting and breathing; yet complex in that you have to face your demons, judgments, and dark emotions without claiming them as yours. When these feelings arise, you let them go and surround yourself with self-compassion, light, and love, ultimately creating more peace. If you begin a practice of meditation gradually, you will begin to feel a more grounded and calm existence.

It is breathing, yoga, and meditation that have allowed me to live a more peaceful and happy life. It has turned my fears into curiosities, anxieties into energy, and triggers into self-compassion. I will end with this quote by Eleanor Roosevelt: **"It isn't enough to talk about peace, one must believe it. And it isn't enough to believe in it, one must work for it."**

I love this because peace is something you have to work for; it does not come easy, at least it hasn't for me. But what I have learned is that some of the best things in my life have come from hard work, patience, and persistence.

PEACE

PURIFY: A purifier's function is to remove contaminants from the air. Being more peaceful will purify contaminants from your body.

What changes can you make in your life to purify the body, and create more peace? Please don't put pressure on yourself—this could be as simple as taking three breathes when your child is having a tantrum, to doing a two-hour yoga class.

pEACE

EDUCATE: Educate yourself on things that cultivate peace. Read and research things that bring peace, and find what resonates with you.

Draw three pictures or write three things you know continually bring you peace?

PECE

ABUNDANCE: Remember there is enough peace for everyone, like the galaxy, it is unending and will never run out.

Spend one minute right now sitting in a space of meditation. Close your eyes, take three deep breaths, and let your body and soul feel the earth's unending abundance of peace. Notice how you feel. Are you more relaxed and peaceful?

PEACE

COMPASSION: It is practically impossible to have peace in your life, without compassion for yourself and others. Compassion is the counterpart to peace.

Write down three ways you can be more compassionate towards yourself, and three ways you can be more compassionate to others, and the world around you.

PEACE

EVOLUTION: Life is always evolving. One day you will feel peaceful and joy, and the next anger and resentment. This is natural and is forever evolving.

Get a piece of paper and with color draw a line down the middle. On one side write what brings you peace, and on the other side write what inhibits you from peace. Put this somewhere so you can be reminded that peace is an evolution, and can revolve around your choices.

Be Grateful

The accept... oneself is the ...ce of ... problem and the ...me of ...

Cracking Open 107

Be Grateful

"Wake at dawn with a winged heart and give thanks for another day of loving."
~Kahlil Gibran

I never experienced gratitude more deeply than when I travelled throughout India. The people I encountered were so grateful for the smallest of gestures, a coin, a crumb of food, or a courteous *"Namaste."* You could feel their hearts light up and whole bodies fill with love. Just being in their presence, I felt a richness of spirit greater than money could ever buy.

Gratitude is appreciation for all that you have in your life.

No matter what your individual troubles may be, it is possible for every human being to experience the essence of gratitude. When you are thankful, you feel less alone and discover a connection to something larger than oneself. When you are feeling gratitude, your load is a little lighter to carry and therefore you are able to carry the load of others. Practicing gratitude fosters compassion for all living beings.

Moreover, cultivating an "attitude of gratitude" has been linked to better health, sounder sleep, less anxiety and depression, higher long-term satisfaction with life, and kinder behavior toward others, including romantic partners. A new study shows that feeling grateful makes people less likely to turn aggressive when provoked. Can it be this simple? All these amazing emotions and feelings for simply being thankful? You betcha.

If we know of all these benefits, why is it so freaking hard to be thankful all the time?

Because when we are in a place of sadness, fear, and anger, the body does not want to go to a place of gratitude, it wants to stay in the "woe is me" space. There are certainly times you need to have a so-called "pity party" after a bad day or setback in life, when you call a friend and say, "I am dying and need to have a fat glass of wine, strong coffee, or a giant piece of chocolate cake and to tell you why my life sucks and I am sad." This process is very important, and I would never suggest removing it from your life.

But what I have found is if you stay in that place too long, you become a victim and begin to drown in your story. One of the greatest life preservers when you are in this negative space is gratitude. Being thankful will bring you back to earth when you are feeling your failures, foibles, and fears. Instead of letting your mind focus on how your life is a mess let me tell you this is easy to do — try to go back to the road of gratitude, focusing on who and what you have in your life that is good and pure. As life coach and self-help author Anthony Robbins says, **"When you are grateful fear disappears and abundance appears."** Let it wake you from your slumber of sadness and remind you about how much support and how many blessings you have traveling through this challenging experience we call life.

I see this brilliantly displayed by my dear friend, Hilary, who is battling cancer. Despite inevitably feeling scared, lost, and sick, she continues to send notes stating how grateful she is for all her love and support and to share photos of her country western dancing, explaining how thankful she is that her body can still move even though it is full of chemo drugs. Hilary is not allowing herself to be suffocated by cancer; she is finding joy and gratitude in her world, even with cancer.

If you sat today or everyday looking at your life without a label of good or bad, but simply in a space of gratitude, how do you think you would walk around in the world? Take a moment and be grateful for the people in your life who give you joy and the magnificence of how your body works and the love you feel for your family and friends. In this state of gratitude, you will most likely experience more delight and appreciation for yourself and this world.

One ritual I have is that every night, as I am slowly falling asleep, I thank God that my children are asleep safe and sound, that the world is still in one piece, that my husband and I have jobs to feed our family, and I have my health. "Let gratitude be the pillow upon which you kneel to say your nightly prayer," says Maya Angelou. I remember how living in a state of gratitude keeps me present in abundance versus depletion, in love versus hate, and in appreciation for the joy of simple moments. And as my eyelids are drooping and my heartbeat is slowing down, I often find myself saying,

Namaste, gracias, and thank you, oh, thank you.

Thanks

TRANSFORMATION: Trust that gratitude will transform pain into pleasure, being lost into being loved, and feeling depleted into feeling dynamic.

Use one color to write down your negative thoughts, and beliefs. Then use a different color to write down what you are grateful for. Notice the difference in your body as you write those two lists in two different colors.

T**H**ANKS

HEART: This is where gratitude lives. When you are feeling lost or as if your world is falling apart, go to the heart to refill your tank of gratitude.

Stop for one minute, put down your pen, and put your hand on your heart. Spend 30 seconds saying what you are grateful for in your life. This may feel awkward or uncomfortable, but notice the lightness you feel when you spend time in your heart, versus your head.

THANKS

AFRAID: It is strange, but it is almost as if people are afraid to live in a state of gratitude, to be really happy. Sometimes it is so much easier to complain, than be thankful. Try to go against the tide, and live with gratitude.

What inhibits you from feeling grateful every day?

Draw or paint a picture of what is stopping you from living in a state of gratitude.

THA**N**KS

NIRVANA: When you practice gratitude, you will attain a deeper state of nirvana. Nirvana is a profound peace of mind, free from suffering.

How can you today, or this week, be in a state of nirvana?

THAN**K**S

KISS: Let your touch transform your heart. Be grateful you have someone to kiss, be it a person, or a pet.

Today kiss your children, partner, neighbor, or friend. Observe the difference
in your soul from just a simple kiss.

THANK

SACRED: When you spend time in a sacred space, be that a church, temple, mosque, or nature, you are more apt to feel grateful. It may be about the space, but I believe gratitude is born when we take time to be quiet and still.

This week find time to go to a space that feels sacred to you.

"Gratitude is the fairest blossom which springs from the soul"

-Henry Ward Beecher

Be Free

Cracking Open 117

Be Free

"Emancipate yourselves from mental slavery, none but ourselves can free our minds."
~Bob Marley

One day I was reading the *New York Times* and saw this headline: "Stuck Ship Breaks Free Near Antarctica." The article went on to document how a Chinese ship holding 52 passengers, the *Xue Long*, had been icebound for several weeks. Fortunately, shifting winds had finally opened a path for the research ship to free itself. This story was fascinating, and I was relieved for all the people on board who were rescued and no longer trapped in the middle of frozen Antarctica, but what struck me the most was the word, "STUCK." From my years as a therapist, I know how easy it is to get stuck in our minds, and how debilitating it is when we get fastened in our own stories and negative thoughts. This chapter is about freeing yourself from that pattern.

I believe the moment you made the choice to buy this book you began to Be Free.

You bought this journal, opened it up, and decided to start reading, writing, contemplating, questioning, and, ultimately, transforming. Somewhere deep down inside, you knew you wanted to create more happiness in your life, to embrace joy in a different way. You wanted to walk in the world with more light and acceptance around your weight, your job, your marriage, or your family. You could not live anymore in a place of fear, with no voice, hindered by low self-esteem or lack of confidence.

You may or may not have been too scared or intimidated to try therapy, workshops, seminars, or conferences, but this journal looked inviting, so you bought it and you opened it and you are finishing it. But here is the thing about life: we are never really finished. Life continues to have its peaks and valleys. We are on a journey. Hopefully this invitation to crack open will become part of your every day life and you will continue to use tools and exercises to advance your internal process of change. You will continue to question or wonder about why you chose to eat ten cookies versus one. Why you let a friend, or someone you thought was a friend, treat you unkindly and did not speak up for yourself? Why you kept saying yes to something that you really wanted to say no to, be that a dinner party, date, or your drug of choice? Understanding your motivations will help you keep on the path to change, and accepting your mistakes and imperfections will give you the courage to be vulnerable, real, and raw and from this place you can be set free

This freedom continues to take work.

You may feel the high of freedom one day and then the next a dark cloud may cover your sunshine. You will need to crack open again and reach into your toolbox of restoration again, be that a walk in the woods, yoga, meditation, a phone call to a friend or family member, a deep dark cry, or simply a fat bowl of popcorn, butter and all. It is impossible to get to the light without going into the dark. I don't care what you choose, but make sure that it is something that can fill your heart versus deplete your soul. You will remind yourself yet again that, "This too shall pass."

Voltaire once said, **"Man is free the moment he wishes to be."** I know a woman who has everything anyone could ever ask for, unlimited amounts of money, beauty, health, children and grandchildren who love her, and friends who want to support her, but she is not free. She is imprisoned by her fears. She cannot see outside of her pain to realize that there is freedom at her fingertips. Alternatively, I met a woman in India to whom I brought food everyday before going to hear the teachings of the Dalai Lama. This woman was disfigured by leprosy, homeless, uneducated, and had no family, but was full of light and freedom. I saw this liberation in her expansive smile and felt it emanating from her joyous spirit. From the outside her external circumstances were dire, but inside she was full of wealth, inner peace, and tranquility. Her freedom came from gratitude, presence, and acceptance of self.

Real freedom is about not labeling relationships or experiences "good" or "bad," but about allowing yourself to be present in every moment. Buddha believed that freedom is about exploring each present moment and each conscious choice. So make a conscious choice today to be free. Let go of the illusion of control. Being truly free means not worrying about the future or having regrets about the past. To live an awakened life you must be in the here and now because your thoughts about the past and future are based in fear. As the poet Haviz says, **"Fear is the cheapest room in the house."**

One day I came home and there was a small package on my doorstep. As I opened the gift I found a rock, I actually laughed out loud thinking that one of my friends was playing a joke on me, but then I saw a card that read, "There is a rough-looking round shaped rock that has a hollow center with beautiful quartz crystals inside; this rock is called a geode. Geodes were formed millions of years ago when the Earth's crust was still in a molten state.

The only way to discover its crystals is to crack it open."

Genius, I thought, pure genius. This is it! Life can look hard and rough on the outside, but if you are willing to crack it open, you will find your find your crystals, jewels, and gems. For a happier life, I want you to crack open; I want you to be free.

I will leave you with one last exercise. I want you to notice how you are feeling at this moment and then simply take three deep breaths and say to yourself, "I am free, I am free, I am free." After taking three seconds to slow down, let go, and not be caught in the web of the mind, you will crack open to what is in front of you, become more awakened to your deepest calling, and be able to continue your pilgrimage of freedom. I know you can do this. I have all the faith in the world that you can walk in the world with less weight on your shoulders and more luminosity in your heart. Stay awake, create openness, dream bigger than before, trust in your process that spending time in the dark will crack open your life to light, let yourself be vulnerable, use your voice, and allow your beauty to be seen by all. I give you permission. I dare you. I want to watch you grow in all your glory.

"The prison door is wide open already. So, why do you remain inside?"
-Rumi

FREE

FEARLESSNESS: Freedom comes from the courage of being able to look at your life without fear.

What is inhibiting you from total freedom? How has fear imprisoned you from becoming freer?

FREE

REBORN: Each moment is the birth of a new beginning. Each day repeat this mantra, "I will Crack Open again and again." Allow the old patterns, and behaviors that are not serving you anymore die in order to create space to be reborn.

What thoughts, and stories, are you holding onto that are inhibiting you from being free?

FREE

EXCITEMENT: You have just accomplished an amazing task. You took hours, and days, to commit to change, to crack old habits, and to wake up to what your life could really be.

Allow yourself to be excited for this amazing transformation of freedom. Share with me how you have transformed from working and reading this journal?

FREE

EMBRACE: I encourage you to sit back, relax, and give yourself some time to embrace all the information, and transformation that is soaking into your body.

Share, draw, doodle, dance, paint, and sing all the ways you have grown on this journey.

A gift for you...

"Ring the bells that still can ring
Forget your perfect offering
There is a crack in everything
That's how the light gets in."
-Leonard Cohen, Anthem

CPSIA information can be obtained at www.ICGtesting.com
Printed in the USA
BVOW05s0416080816

457816BV00038B/105/P